MARS

Heather DiLorenzo Williams
and Warren Rylands

Go to **www.eyediscover.com** and enter this book's unique code.

BOOK CODE

AVW55596

EYEDISCOVER brings you optic readalongs that support active learning.

Published by AV² by Weigl
350 5th Avenue, 59th Floor New York, NY 10118
Website: www.eyediscover.com

Copyright ©2019 AV² by Weigl
All rights reserved. No part of this publication may be reproduced, stored in a retrieval system, or transmitted in any form or by any means, electronic, mechanical, photocopying, recording, or otherwise, without the prior written permission of the publisher.

Library of Congress Control Number: 2018953516

ISBN 978-1-4896-8009-9 (hardcover)

Printed in Brainerd, Minnesota,United States
1 2 3 4 5 6 7 8 9 0 22 21 20 19 18

082018
120917

Project Coordinators: John Willis
Designer: Mandy Christiansen

Weigl acknowledges Alamy, Getty Images, and Shutterstock as the primary image suppliers for this title.

EYEDISCOVER provides enriched content, optimized for tablet use, that supplements and complements this book. EYEDISCOVER books strive to create inspired learning and engage young minds in a total learning experience.

Watch
Video content brings each page to life.

Browse
Thumbnails make navigation simple.

Read
Follow along with text on the screen.

Listen
Hear each page read aloud.

Your EYEDISCOVER Optic Readalongs come alive with...

Audio
Listen to the entire book read aloud.

Video
High resolution videos turn each spread into an optic readalong.

OPTIMIZED FOR

- ✔ TABLETS
- ✔ WHITEBOARDS
- ✔ COMPUTERS
- ✔ AND MUCH MORE!

In this book, you will learn about

- what it is
- what it is made of
- what happens there

and much more!

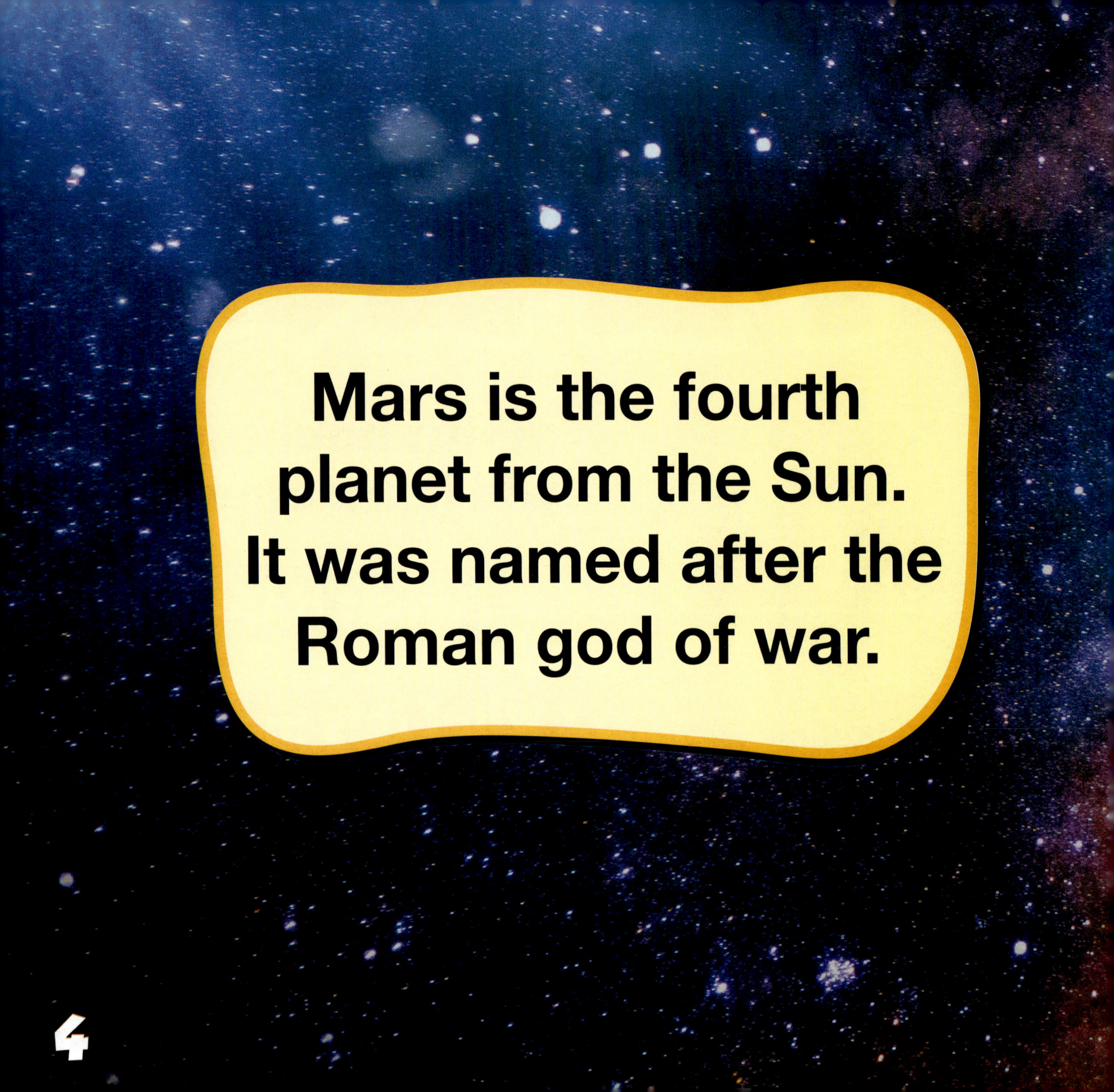

Mars is the fourth planet from the Sun. It was named after the Roman god of war.

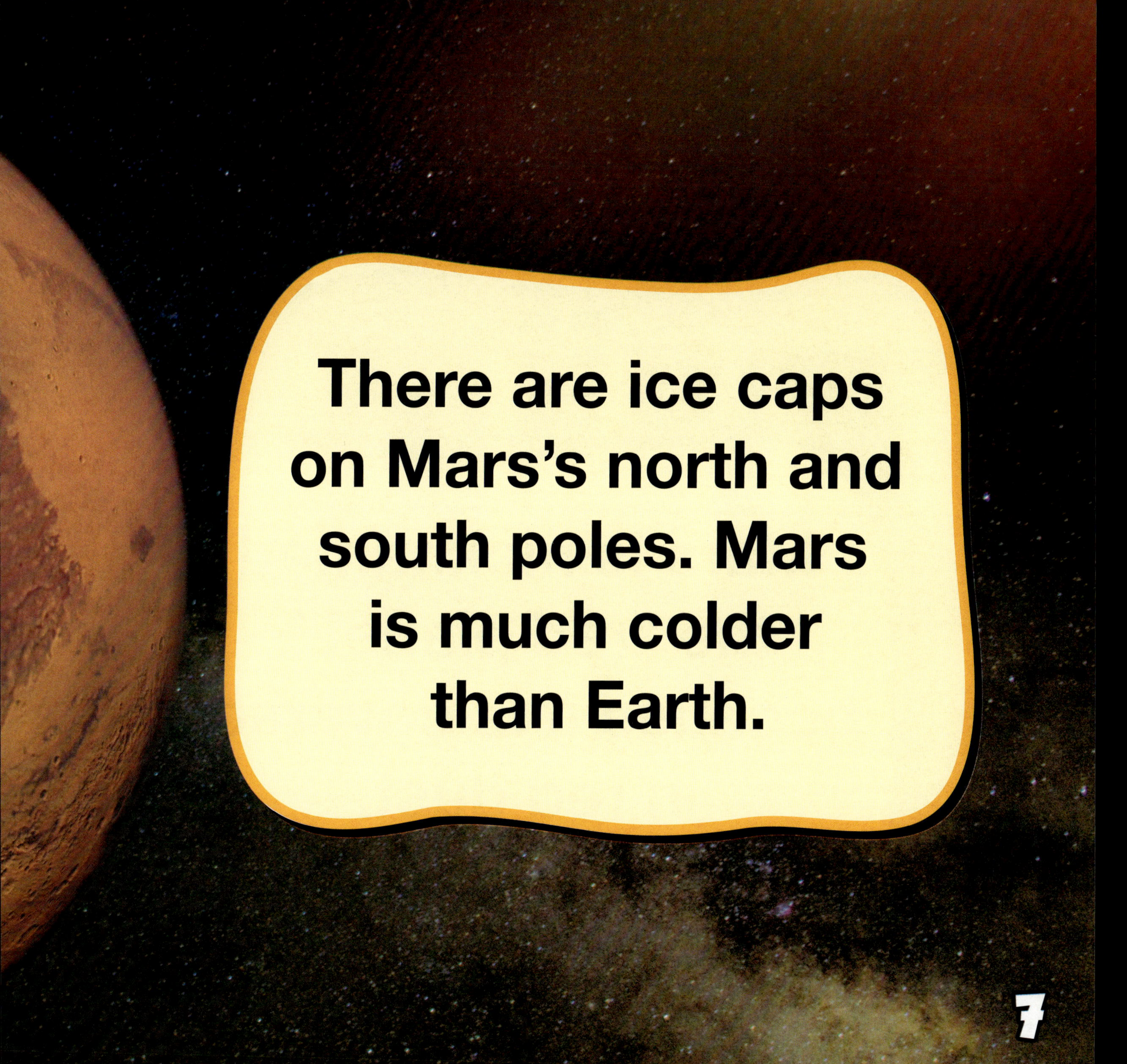

There are ice caps on Mars's north and south poles. Mars is much colder than Earth.

Mars is nicknamed the "red planet" because it is covered in red dust.

Mars has huge dust storms. These storms make the planet's sky look red.

The biggest mountain on Mars is Olympus Mons. It is more than three times higher than Mount Everest.

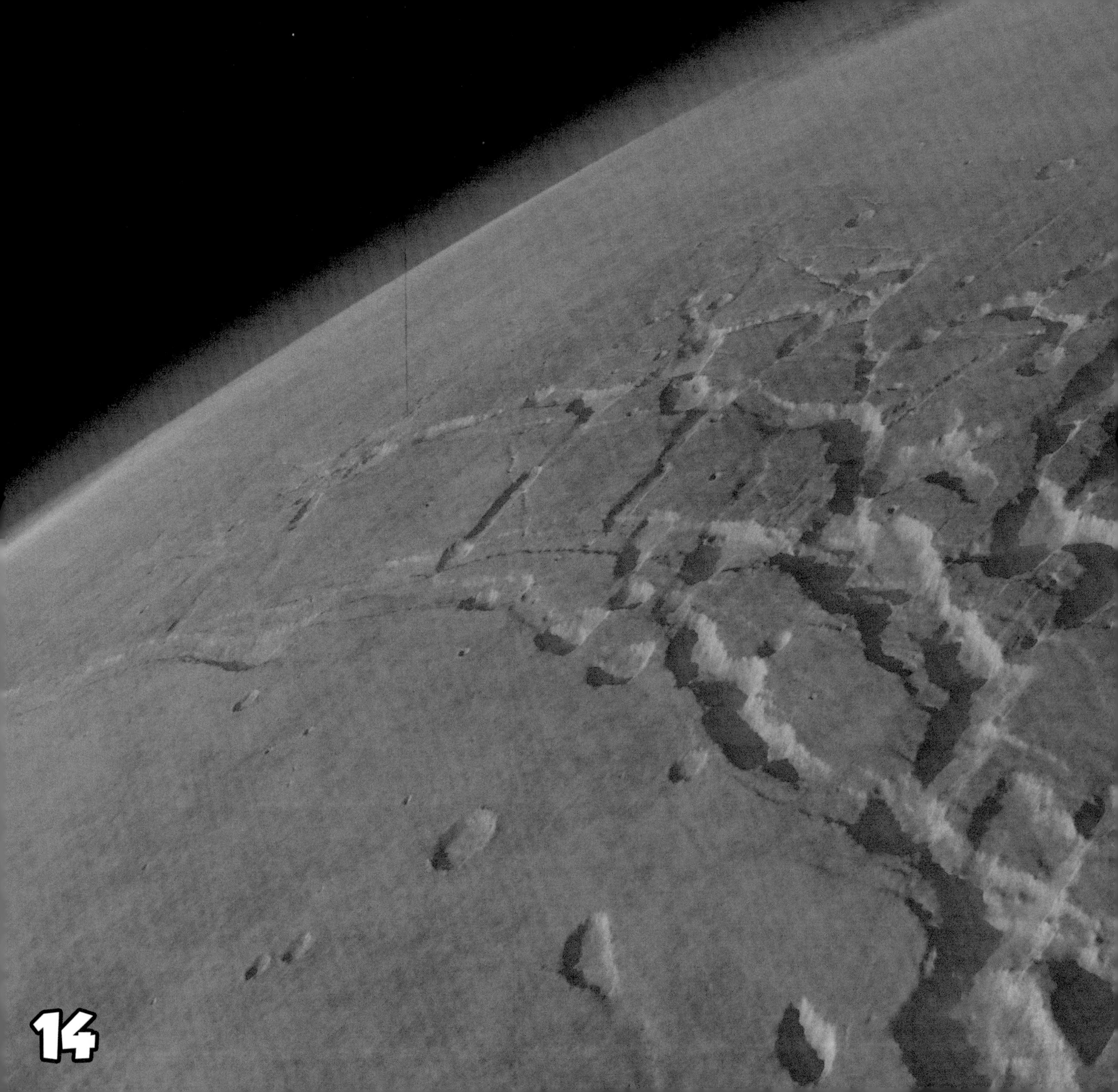
14

Mars has deep canyons. Valles Marineris is the largest canyon in our solar system.

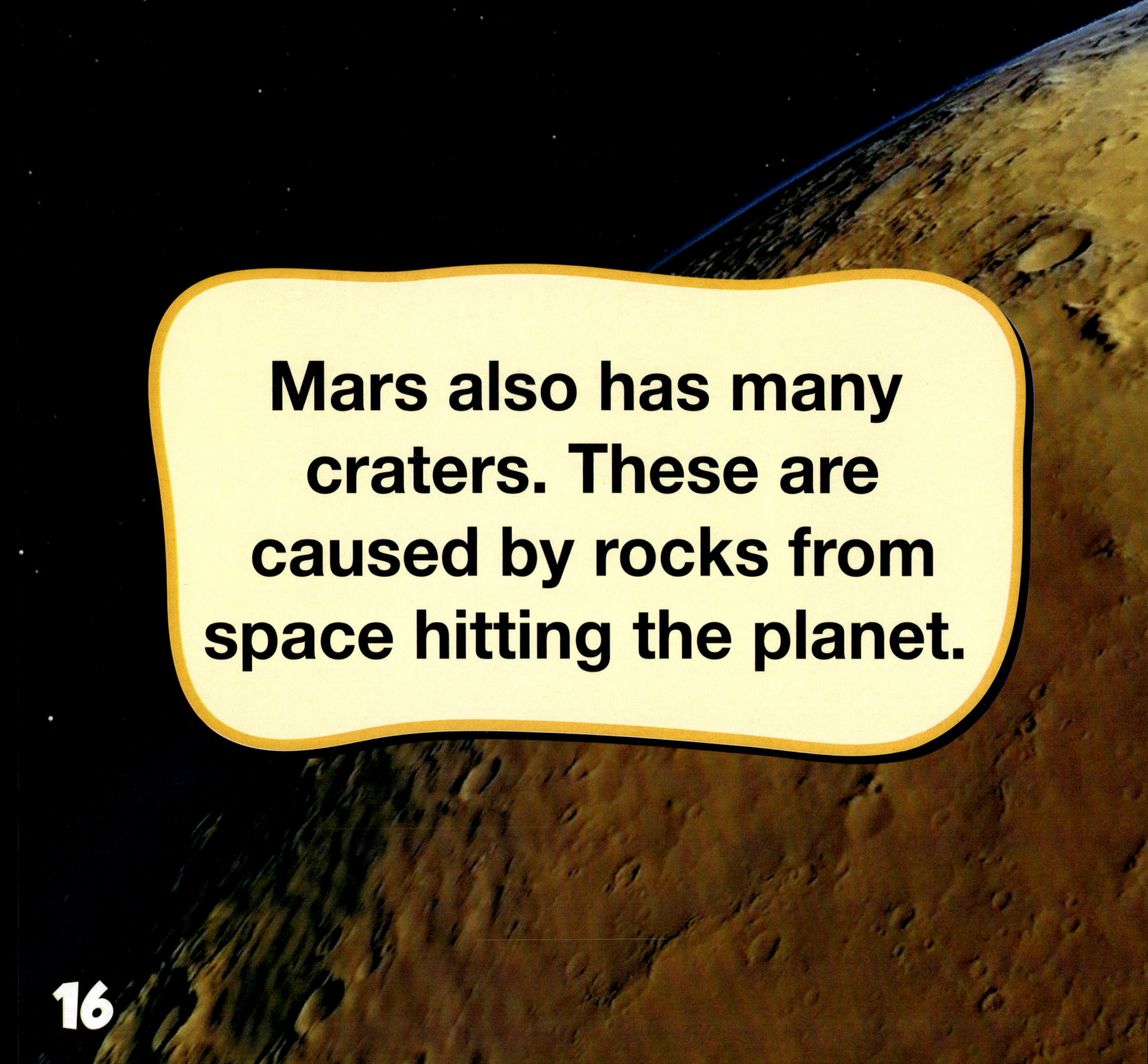

Mars also has many craters. These are caused by rocks from space hitting the planet.

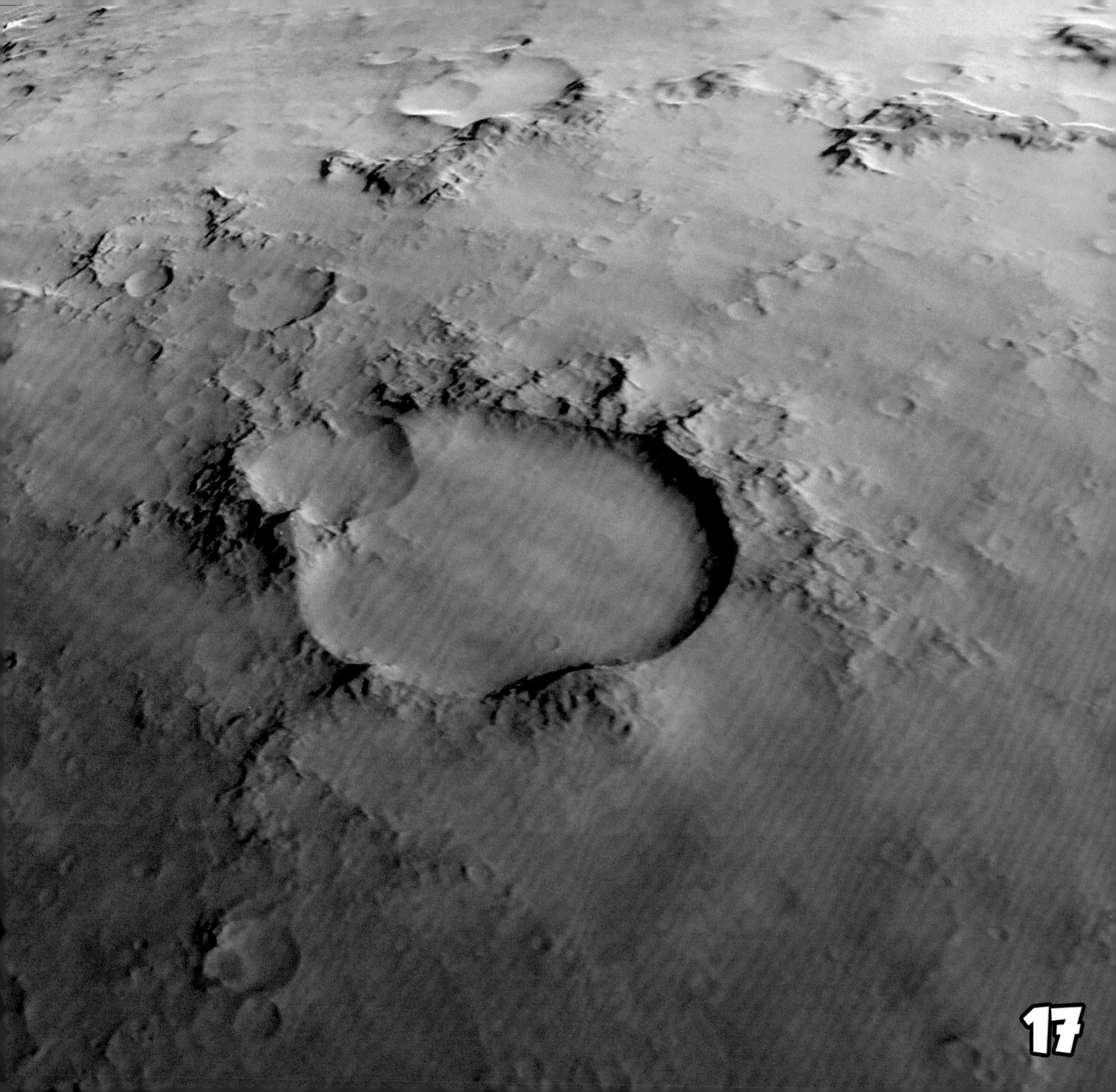

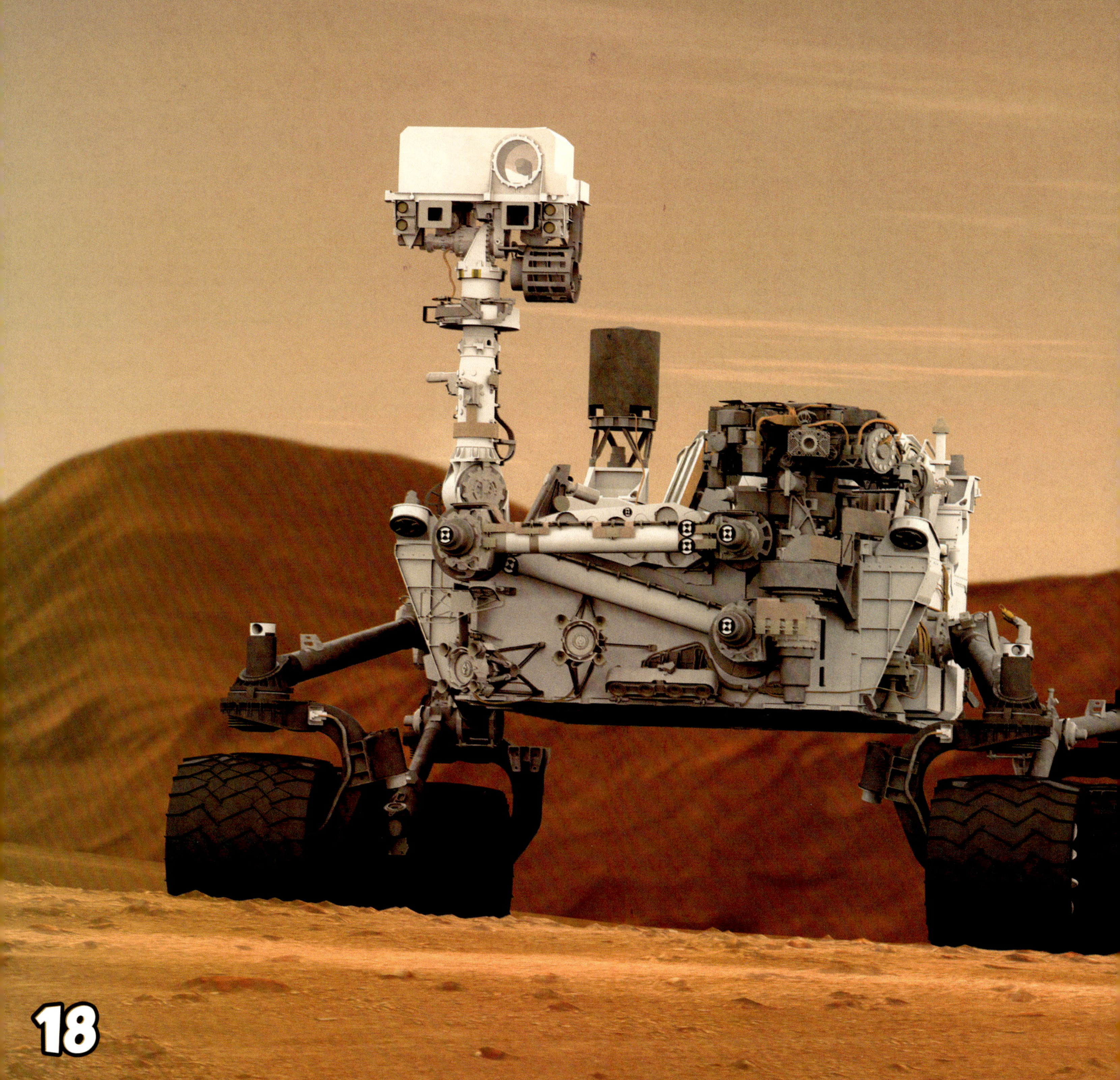

Scientists send machines to explore Mars. The Mars rover *Curiosity* landed on Mars in 2012.

www.nasa.gov/orion
NASA

People are trying to find out how to send humans to Mars. They want to make it safe for humans to visit and live there.

The average temperature on Mars is -67° Fahrenheit.
(-55° Celsius)

More than 43,000 large craters have been found on Mars.

One Mars year is equal to **687** Earth days.

Mars has **two moons** named **Phobos** and **Deimos**.

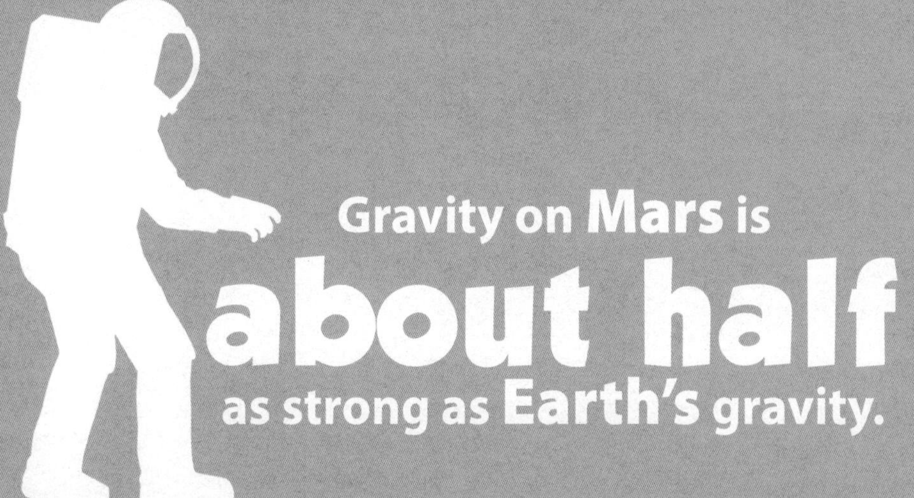

Gravity on **Mars** is **about half** as strong as **Earth's** gravity.

KEY WORDS

Research has shown that as much as 65 percent of all written material published in English is made up of 300 words. These 300 words cannot be taught using pictures or learned by sounding them out. They must be recognized by sight. This book contains 35 common sight words to help young readers improve their reading fluency and comprehension. This book also teaches young readers several important content words, such as proper nouns. These words are paired with pictures to aid in learning and improve understanding.

Page	Sight Words First Appearance
4	after, from, is, it, of, the, was
7	and, are, Earth, much, on, than, there
8	because, in
11	has, look, make, these
12	more, three
15	our
16	also, by, many
19	to
21	find, for, how, live, out, people, they, want

Page	Content Words First Appearance
4	god, Mars, planet, Roman, Sun, war
7	ice caps, north, poles, south
8	dust, red
11	sky, storms
12	mountain, Mount Everest, Olympus Mons
15	canyons, solar system, Valles Marineris
16	craters, rocks
19	Curiosity, machines, rover, scientists
21	humans

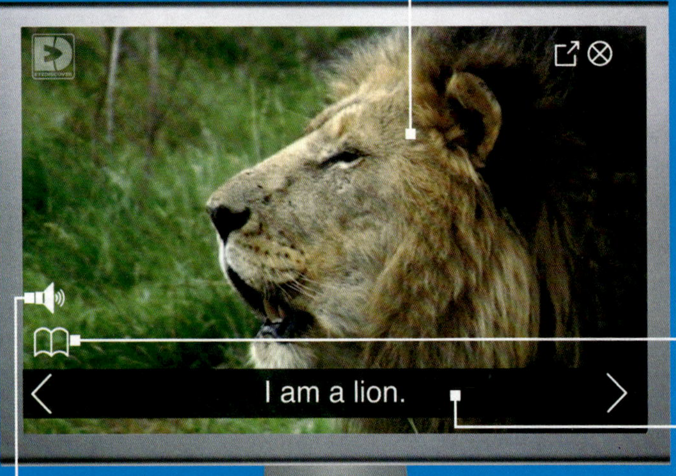

Watch
Video content brings each page to life.

Browse
Thumbnails make navigation simple.

Read
Follow along with text on the screen.

Listen
Hear each page read aloud.

Go to www.eyediscover.com and enter this book's unique code.

BOOK CODE

AVW55596